8/97

msc

A Day in the Life of a...

Farmer

Carol Watson

W

FRANKLIN WATTS

LONDON • NEW YORK • SYDNEY

This is Helen. She is a farmer.
Helen's farm is very large and
she has many fields in which
to grow her crops and keep her animals.

Helen starts her day at 7.30 am when
she talks to her staff at the farmhouse.

Then she sets off in her car to
see how things are getting on
in the different parts of the farm.

First Helen stops off to look at the dairy cows. She checks that they have enough grass to eat and that they are all looking well.

Twice a day the cows
go into the milking
parlour to be milked.

Some of the milk
is kept in milk churns
to give to their calves.

Next Helen goes to visit the pigs. "How are they today?" she asks Daz, the pig man. Daz tells his boss about any pigs that are a problem.

The pigs are of the
'Saddlebacks' breed.
Helen takes her
daughter, Sophie,
and friend, Sam,
to see the arcs
where the pigs live.
They meet the piglets.

"Let's collect some eggs for lunch,"
Helen says to the children. They all
head off to the hen house to see
what they can find.

A hen watches closely as the children peep into the nesting boxes and search through the straw inside.

"Here's one!"
shouts Sam.
"Look, I've found two!"
says Sophie.
"We'll soon have
enough for everyone,"
Helen tells them.

Back at the farmhouse they eat
lunch with the other people who
work on the farm. Helen's husband,
Henry, joins them.

Henry is in charge of all the farm machinery. He keeps the tractors and trailers in good condition and mends them when they go wrong.

Henry is driving one of the tractors. This pulls different machines which plough the earth, cut and pick up the grass, or sow seeds into the soil.

After lunch, Helen visits Hugh, the shepherd. He looks after the 650 sheep that are on the farm.

"This new-born lamb was cold so I've put a jacket on it," he tells Helen.

14

"Go to it, Sedge!" Hugh
tells his sheepdog.
The dog rounds up the
sheep and brings them
close to the shepherd
for inspection.

Next Helen goes field-walking
to see how the crops are growing.
"This wheat looks healthy and strong,"
she says to herself.

One field is full
of clover. "This has
nitrogen in its roots,"
Helen tells the children.

"Nitrogen is good for the soil and
it will make the next crop in this
field grow better."

The last call of the day is to
the farm's shop nearby.
It sells food made from the animals
on Helen's farm. "The ice-cream is
the best!" says Sophie.

18

Helen returns home. She goes to
her office to finish off some work
on the computer. "That's it for today,"
she says. "Time for supper!"

Make a wormery

If you want to grow healthy plants you need to have good soil. Soil is made of lots of different things such as sand, clay, water, air and dead plants. Worms are important for the soil. They mix it up, and help water and air get deep down into the different layers. You can see how worms move through the soil by making a **wormery**.

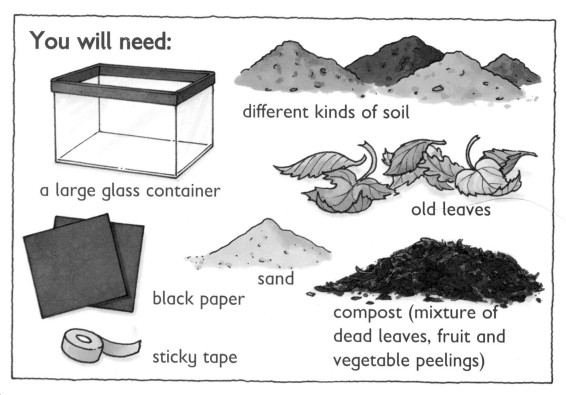

You will need:

a large glass container

different kinds of soil

old leaves

black paper

sand

sticky tape

compost (mixture of dead leaves, fruit and vegetable peelings)

1. Put layers of different soil, sand and compost into the container.

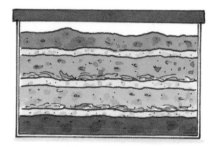

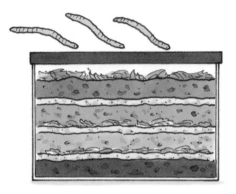

2. Cover with a layer of old leaves and add some worms.

3. Then cover the top and sides with black paper.

4. Add a little water from time to time to keep the container moist.

5. Every few days lift off one side of the paper to see how the worms are, where they are working and how quickly they mix up the layers.

How you can help farmers

1. Keep to the public path when you walk on farmland.

2. Always fasten gates when you go in and out of fields.

3. Don't play or trample on the crops that are growing.

4. Keep your dog on a lead when you see farm animals, especially sheep.

5. Use gates and stiles to cross walls and fences.

6. Be careful of fire.

7. Take your litter home with you.

Facts about farms

There are different kinds of farms. Some grow wheat or vegetables. Others keep animals for meat or grow fruit. Dairy farms keep cows for their milk which makes cheese, butter, cream and yoghurt.

Helen runs an **organic** farm. This means that no chemicals are used to help grow the crops and only occasionally are they used in the rearing of the animals. The animals roam freely in the fields and live a long time before they are killed for their meat. If you want to support organic farmers, ask for organic produce in your supermarket or local shops.

Most farms today are **intensive**. They use **agrochemicals** which help to control the weeds and pests that attack the crops. They also use **inorganic fertilisers** to help the plants grow more quickly. Most of the farm animals live indoors so that the farmer can protect them against disease and fatten them up more quickly. Sometimes they are also given drugs to protect them against disease. Intensive farms are able to produce food more quickly and cheaply than organic farms.

Index

© 1997 Franklin Watts

Franklin Watts
96 Leonard Street
London
EC2A 4RH

Franklin Watts Australia
14 Mars Road
Lane Cove
NSW 2066

UK ISBN: 0 7496 2614 3

Dewey Decimal Classification
Number: 630

10 9 8 7 6 5 4 3 2 1

A CIP catalogue record for this
book is available from the
British Library.

Printed in Malaysia

Editor: Sarah Ridley

Designer: Kirstie Billingham

Photographer:
    Harry Cory-Wright

Illustrator: Kim Woolley

With thanks to Helen Browning
and Sophie Stoye, Sam Finney
and Elizabeth Hobson.